THE FIRST FLYERS

David Jefferis

Illustrated by
Michael Roffe and Ron Jobson

Franklin Watts

London   New York   Toronto   Sydney

First published in 1988 by
Franklin Watts
12a Golden Square
London W1R 4BA

First published in the USA
by Franklin Watts Inc.
387 Park Avenue South
New York, N.Y. 10016

First published in Australia
by Franklin Watts
Australia
14 Mars Road
Lane Cove, NSW 2066

UK ISBN 0 86313 668 0
US ISBN 0-531-10563-6
Library of Congress
Catalog Card No: 87-51696

Technical consultant
Tim Callaway, RAF Museum,
Hendon, London

Designed and produced by
Sunrise Books

© 1988 Franklin Watts

Printed in Belgium

THE FIRST FLYERS

Contents

Introduction

A French doctor, Jean François Pilâtre de Rozier, made the first air flight. His 1783 trip was in a hot air balloon made by the Montgolfier brothers. In the years that followed, balloonists made many ascents but it was not flight in the true sense, as there was no direction control – balloons simply drifted with the wind. Airships powered by steam engines made some progress but were very slow.

The age of flight really began in 1903 when the Wright brothers took to the air in their *Flyer*. Three years after the Wrights' first flight, the best any European aircraft had managed was a 21-second hop. But within a few years aviation was advancing rapidly and long-distance flights lasting many hours had been made.

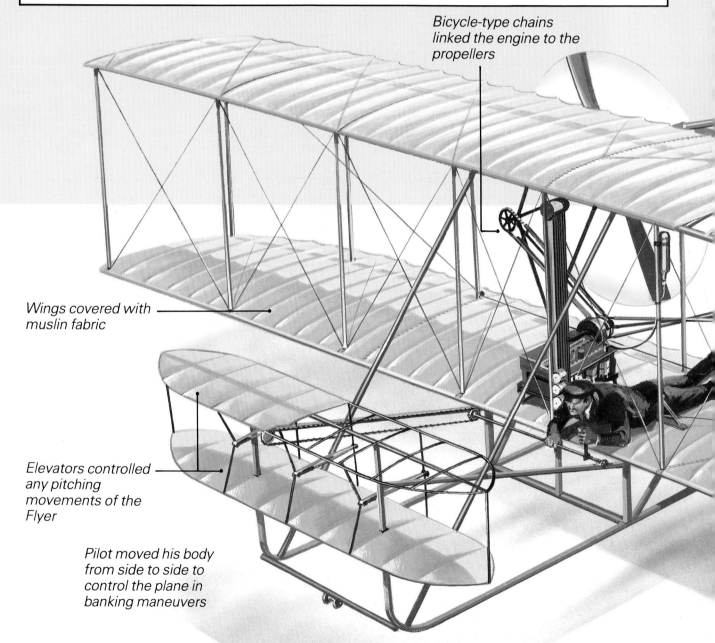

Bicycle-type chains linked the engine to the propellers

Wings covered with muslin fabric

Elevators controlled any pitching movements of the Flyer

Pilot moved his body from side to side to control the plane in banking maneuvers

Pioneer aviators

Wilbur and Orville Wright designed and built the first successful aircraft, the Wright *Flyer*. It was a biplane, made mainly of wood and fabric. Its single engine was built in the workshop of the Wrights' bicycle manufacturing business.

The Wright brothers carried out their flight program carefully, step-by-step. They made calculations, built models and tested them in a specially built wind tunnel. Then they checked the results in the air. The *Flyer* was the successful result of several years of flight research.

Though modern aircraft are vastly more complex than the *Flyer*, the designers of today follow much the same basic research principles as those of the Wright brothers.

Twin rudders

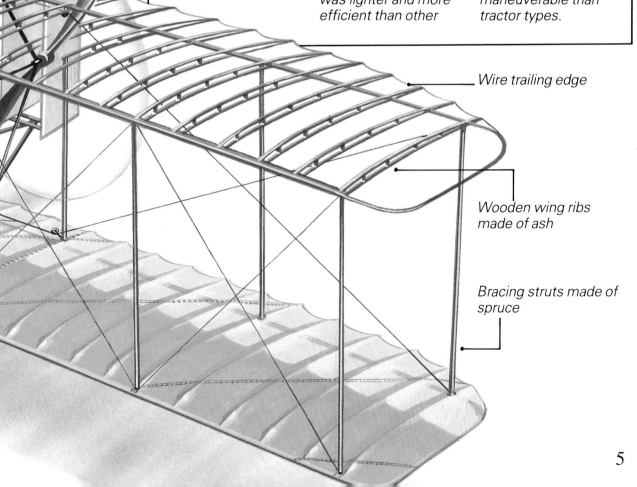

▽ Orville Wright took the Flyer into the air on December 17, 1903. This first flight, just 37 m (121 ft) long, took the Wright brothers into the history books – for this was the first successful flight by a heavier-than-air machine.

The development of the internal combustion engine in the late 19th century made powered flight possible. Steam engines were too heavy for the job. The Wright brothers designed their own engine for the Flyer. It was lighter and more efficient than other petrol engines of the time. Two propellers pushed the Flyer through the air. "Tractor" propellers mounted in front became popular in World War I – the extra structure needed by pusher planes made them slower and less maneuverable than tractor types.

Wire trailing edge

Wooden wing ribs made of ash

Bracing struts made of spruce

The dream of flight

△ Bird flight looks easy and effortless. But to flap hard enough for takeoff and flight, a human would need immense chest and shoulder muscles. Even if flight was possible, a tail would be needed to control in-flight maneuvers.

For thousands of years, people have wanted to be like the birds and fly through the air.

There are many legends of early flights and one of the most ancient is the Greek myth of Daedalus and his son Icarus. To escape from the island of Crete where they were imprisoned, Daedalus made two pairs of wings. He warned Icarus not to fly too high, since the wax which held the wings together might melt in the heat of the sun. Icarus ignored his father's instructions and soared upward. The wax melted, the wings came apart and Icarus plummeted to his death in the sea. According to the legend, Daedalus flew on to Sicily. This was only a story but even so, to many would-be aviators, imitating the wing motion of birds seemed the obvious way to fly.

For hundreds of years, advances in aviation were limited to jumps from towers or other high points, using cloaks as parachutes or homemade wings to glide.

Unfortunately, most flying attempts ended with bruises, broken bones or even death. People had yet to learn that human beings do not have strong enough muscles to fly like birds. No matter how hard these would-be aeronauts flapped, there was no chance of a successful flight.

Flight before the aeroplane

◁ Kites were invented by the Chinese. The diamond kite became common in Europe during the early 18th century.

◁ On November 21, 1783, two Frenchmen flew 8 km (5 miles) in a Montgolfier hot air balloon. De Rozier (who had earlier made a tethered flight) and the Marquis d'Arlandes reached a height of 900 m (3,000 ft) during their flight.

△ In the 18th century, the Marquis de Bacqueville tried to fly across the River Seine in Paris. He crashed and injured himself.

◁ Sir George Cayley made this model glider in the early 19th century. It had a wing, a slender fuselage and a tailplane.

Gliding experiments

△ Cayley's triplane of 1849 was equipped with a three-wheel undercarriage, a boat-like fuselage and a movable tailplane for steering. Flights were made downhill and by pulling the triplane on a rope like a kite. The coachman's glider was a monoplane design. Aside from his gliders George Cayley invented hot-air engines, caterpillar tracks (as used on tanks), artificial limbs and other devices.

Sir George Cayley was a brilliant aeronautical pioneer of the 19th century. He realized that trying to copy the flapping wings of birds was a waste of time. Better and simpler, he thought, to look at the steady, outstretched gliding wings of a soaring bird such as a gull or an albatross.

Cayley spent much of his life experimenting with model aircraft and gliders. In 1849, when he was 76, his full-scale triplane design was rolled down a slope with a 10-year-old boy aboard as a passenger. The triplane

Otto Lilienthal

Otto Lilienthal was a German engineer who became one of the great air pioneers. He started flying in 1891, and by 1894 he had made many successful gliding flights.

His machines were hang gliders with no moving parts, and he swung his body and legs to control his flight. His career came to a tragic end on August 9, 1896, when a gust of wind caught his glider. He side-slipped into the ground, broke his back and died the next day.

floated off the ground and glided for several yards before touching down again safely. Another short flight was made later, the triplane being pulled against the wind on a rope.

Four years later, Cayley sent one of his coachmen on a gliding flight over the grounds of Brompton Hall, Cayley's home in Yorkshire. Cayley's granddaughter, who watched the event, wrote of the machine "I think it came down rather a shorter distance than expected." Even so, the coachman hurriedly got himself clear of the machine once it had come to a halt and promptly quit his job, saying "I was hired to drive and not to fly."

Cayley realized that to take off and fly any great distance, an aircraft needed a small but powerful engine. The only power source available in Cayley's time was steam. And steam engines were too cumbersome and heavy. But his basic idea, that of aircraft as powered gliders, remains true for every aircraft that has ever flown.

The first powered takeoffs

The very first powered aircraft to leave the ground was a spidery contraption designed by the Frenchman Félix du Temple. In 1874, his steam-powered craft became airborne for a few moments after a run down a sloping ramp – not a true flight, but a good attempt.

Sixteen years later another Frenchman, Clément Ader, was ready to test his *Eole*, a bat-winged single-seat flying machine. On October 9, 1890, vapor hissing from its specially designed steam engine, the *Eole* chugged into the air for a distance of

about 50 m (165 ft). Most of the short hop was little more than 20 cm (8 in) off the ground. The *Eole* had no steering controls and could not maintain its flight for long, so while it left the ground under its own power, the event could not be counted as a flight under full control.

Other aircraft that managed short hops included a steam-powered biplane designed by Sir Hiram Maxim, inventor of the machine gun. This craft left the support rails of a test rig in 1894. The Russians claimed a first some 21 years earlier. In 1884, a monoplane designed

▷ *Ader's Eole on its grasshopping flight of 1890. The aircraft had folding wings for easier transportation. Ader designed two more aircraft but one remained uncompleted, while the other was not as good as the Eole.*

by Alexander Mozhaiski left the ground for a few seconds after a run down a ski-jump ramp. But the main problem all these aircraft shared was that they were far too heavy – they all depended on cumbersome steam engines for power.

△ Félix du Temple's aircraft of 1874 had a pair of forward-swept wings. It had a large rudder for steering and a rear-mounted elevator to pitch the craft up or down. Earlier, in 1857, du Temple had built a flying model aircraft powered by a clockwork motor, later replaced with a small steam engine. Though only a model, it could keep itself up in the air, the first to do so.

Flight at last

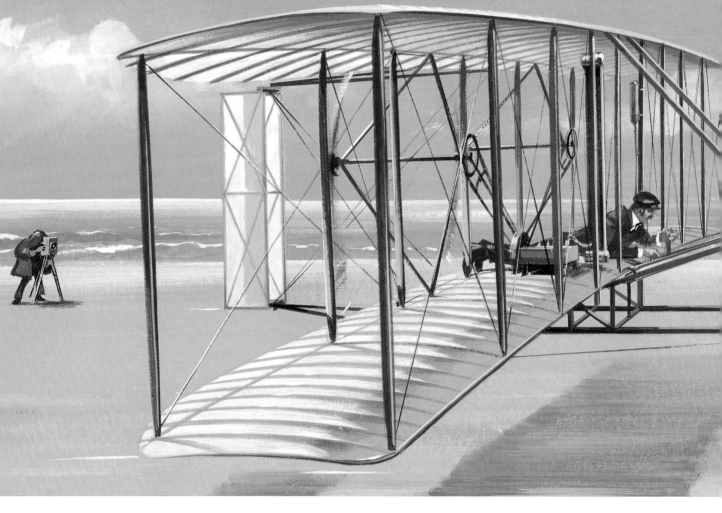

Wilbur and Orville Wright became seriously interested in flying after they learnt of the tragic death of Otto Lilienthal in 1896.

Inspired by Lilienthal's flights, the Wrights experimented with model planes and various gliders for seven years before their first powered flying machine, the *Flyer*, was ready. The Wrights owned a bicycle manufacturing business which provided them with the money they needed for the expensive research work.

On December 14, 1903, the *Flyer* was taken to the Kill Devil Hills in North Carolina to begin flight tests.

Winning the toss of a coin, Wilbur climbed aboard as first pilot. The engine roared and the *Flyer* left the ground, only to rear up, lose lift and crash. But Wilbur was unhurt and the *Flyer* was not too badly damaged.

By Thursday December 17, the *Flyer* was repaired, the weather was good and the Wrights were ready to try again. It was now Orville's turn to be pilot. Propellers spinning, the *Flyer* roared down the takeoff track and made a 12-second hop. The brothers made three more flights that day. Orville sent a telegram to his father which read: SUCCESS FOUR

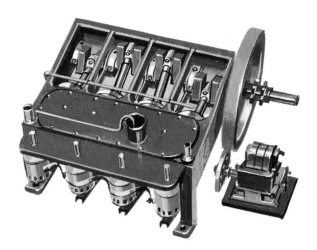

◁ The Flyer took off from a special test track to keep its wooden skids from plowing into the soft sand. The first flight took place just after 10.35 on the morning of December 17, 1903.

△ The Wrights built their own engine for the Flyer as no motor car engine was light enough. The engine was mounted on the lower wing, to the right of the pilot, who lay in the middle.

FLIGHTS THURSDAY MORNING ALL AGAINST TWENTY ONE MILE WIND STARTED FROM LEVEL WITH ENGINE POWER ALONE AVERAGE SPEED THROUGH AIR THIRTY ONE MILES LONGEST 57 SECONDS INFORM PRESS HOME CHRISTMAS. The 57 was a mistake in transmission – the longest flight was actually 59 seconds.

Many of the newspapers ignored the news or treated it as a joke, but that didn't change the fact that the Wright brothers had conquered the air. The age of flight had begun.

Samuel Langley was a famous American scientist who designed a twin-wing plane, the Aerodrome. The spindly-looking plane was launched twice from the roof of a houseboat on the Potomac river, in October and November 1903. It crashed both times, which was why the Wrights' achievement was ignored by many newspapers – the press had a good time poking fun at Langley's failures and treated the whole idea of flight as a fantasy.

13

Aircraft design

The early years of aviation were a time of much experimenting. There were no rules to say where wings, engines, fins or rudders should be placed, or even how many there should be.

The Wrights were far in advance of European ideas and had come up with an excellent basic design in their *Flyer*, but other pioneer aviators tried all sorts of layouts and designs, with varying degrees of success.

On these pages are three design approaches. The Phillips Multiplane had wings like venetian blinds but was written off by its designer after a few disappointing hops. The *14-bis* was a little better and made the first official flights in Europe at the end of 1906, but its longest flight was just 21 seconds.

The Antoinette of 1908 was much more successful. It was one of the first single-wing or monoplane designs, a layout which has remained standard for most of the history of flight. Biplanes became popular for a time, especially during World War I, since ill-founded reports after a series of accidents suggested that monoplanes were not as strong as braced biplanes.

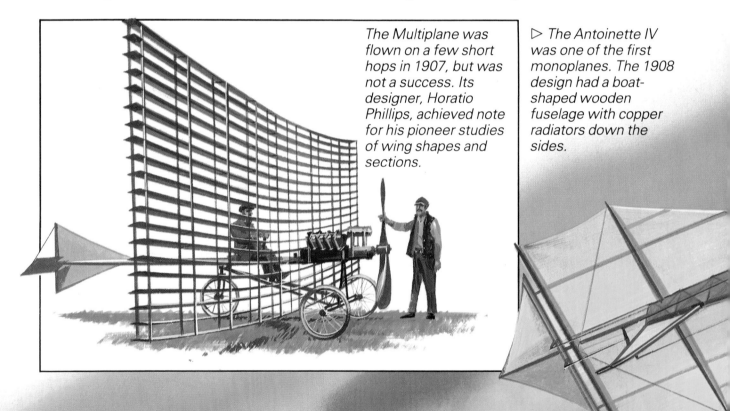

The Multiplane was flown on a few short hops in 1907, but was not a success. Its designer, Horatio Phillips, achieved note for his pioneer studies of wing shapes and sections.

▷ The Antoinette IV was one of the first monoplanes. The 1908 design had a boat-shaped wooden fuselage with copper radiators down the sides.

The 14-bis looked like a box-kite. In 1906 its designer, Alberto Santos-Dumont, made the first European flights in the aircraft. Like the Wright Flyer, the 14-bis flew ''tail-first.'' It also had its rudder in front.

Flying in Europe

The first person to fly an aircraft in Europe was a Brazilian millionaire inventor, Alberto Santos-Dumont, who went to Paris where he aimed to become the world's first flyer.

After experimenting with some very successful airships, Santos-Dumont made the first European flight in a clumsy-looking plane, which looked like several box kites tied together. He first flew the *14-bis* in 1906, some three years after the Wright brothers' first flight. But many people in France didn't believe that the Wrights could be so far ahead of European efforts and for a time, Santos-Dumont thought he was the world's first air pilot.

Santos-Dumont's ideas went beyond such first flights – he wanted to build a cheap plane that anyone could fly, a "people's plane." And with his tiny Demoiselle he got quite close to that aim. The 1909 plane was cheap to buy and easy to fly. The plane was, however, overshadowed by bigger and faster aircraft developed by rivals such as Louis Blériot (who became famous for crossing the English Channel) and Henry Farman.

In 1908 Farman had become one of the most famous aviators by flying the first circular flight in Europe. This was considered a major breakthrough at a time when anything other than a straight-line flight on a calm day was thought to be risky.

In the summer of 1908, Wilbur Wright came from the United States to demonstrate to stunned Europeans what control in the air was all about.

▷ *The Demoiselle (Dragonfly) was reckoned as the world's lightest aircraft by Britain's Flight magazine, weighing little more than 91kg (200lb).*

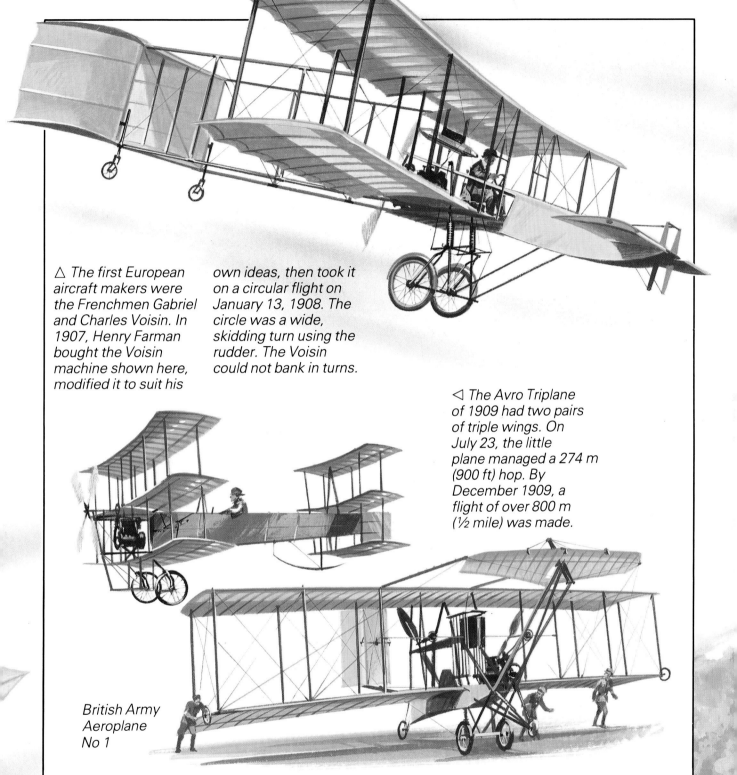

△ The first European aircraft makers were the Frenchmen Gabriel and Charles Voisin. In 1907, Henry Farman bought the Voisin machine shown here, modified it to suit his own ideas, then took it on a circular flight on January 13, 1908. The circle was a wide, skidding turn using the rudder. The Voisin could not bank in turns.

◁ The Avro Triplane of 1909 had two pairs of triple wings. On July 23, the little plane managed a 274 m (900 ft) hop. By December 1909, a flight of over 800 m (½ mile) was made.

British Army Aeroplane No 1

△ Britain's first pilot was "Colonel" Samuel Cody who came from Texas. King George V once mistakenly thought he was "Buffalo Bill" Cody of the US Cavalry, after which Samuel Cody made everyone use the rank! Around 1900, Samuel Cody started experimenting with man-lifting kites. The British Army was interested and by 1906 Cody's kites were used by the Royal Engineers. Cody's next idea was to build an aircraft. In 1908 his British Army Aeroplane No 1 left the ground at Farnborough, making Cody the first aviator in Britain. Cody crashed after a flight of 424 m (1,390 ft) but he survived to build another biplane the following year.

Control in the air

The Wright brothers were the first aviators to be able to control their machines safely in flight. In 1908, Wilbur Wright flew a Type A in France and he impressed the spectators by smoothly rolling, banking and turning the plane in figure-eights.

The Wrights used wing-warping for roll control. Cables twisted the rear edges of the wingtips up or down to roll the aircraft from side to side. Downwarp raised a wing, upwarp lowered it.

Like the *Flyer*, the Type A had a front-mounted elevator which tilted up and down to change the angle of the nose. A blend of wing-warp to roll gently into a turn, combined with a touch of rudder to steady any yawing, would result in a smooth change of direction. A light pressure on the elevator control could make this a climbing or descending turn.

Aircraft of today use much the same system of flight control but separate flaps, called ailerons, long ago replaced wing-warping.

△ The Type A had three flight controls. An elevator stick was placed by the instructor's left knee. He sat on the left. A combined wing-warp and rudder stick was placed between the two seats, and the pupil's elevator stick was by his right knee.

Aircraft today link the elevator and ailerons as a single stick or control wheel. The rudder is operated by foot pedals.

Takeoff and landing in a Wright Type A

▽ The Type A was usually launched by catapult.

First a weight was raised up a small tower by a team of eager helpers. A tow rope was then attached to the aircraft by a team of helpers.

▽ The weight was released, and its attached rope pulled the Type A along its takeoff track. Wilbur angled the elevator up to lift the nose and let go the tow rope. The Type A flew off at a shallow angle.

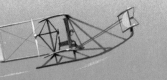

▽ For a smooth landing, Wilbur pushed the left stick to lower the elevator and so drop the nose. Near the ground, Wilbur eased back the elevator to bring the nose level. The Type A sank toward the ground.

▽ Just before touchdown. Wilbur raised the nose a little to "flare" the plane. This created a cushion of air to soften the landing. The engine was shut down, the plane touched down and bumped to a halt.

Louis Blériot

Before dawn on July 25, 1909, French aviator Louis Blériot and his business partner Alfred Le Blanc drove from their hotel in Calais, France, to the garage where a small monoplane, the Blériot *No XI* was stored.

Louis Blériot's aim was to fly the English Channel, an overwater flight of 37 km (23 miles). Though a short distance, it was a major challenge to the fragile and unreliable aircraft of 1909, so much so that the London Daily Mail newspaper offered a large prize to the first aviator to make the crossing.

At 4.00 am, *No XI* was ready for takeoff. In the predawn light, Blériot gave the plane a short test flight, then landed to wait for dawn since the rules of the Daily Mail stated that the flight had to be between sunrise and sunset of the same day. By 4.30 am the sun was up and five minutes later Blériot roared off, at full power to clear some telegraph wires. He headed west, over the Channel toward England. A French

On July 19, 1909, Englishman Hubert Latham made the first Channel crossing attempt in an Antoinette. Engine failure a few minutes after takeoff brought him down in the water. He was unhurt and was soon rescued by a French ship.

navy destroyer, the *Escopette*, was down below steaming along to escort him, but flying at 72 km/h (45 mph) he soon overtook it.

As the ship passed behind, Blériot lost sight of it – and everything else too, except sea and sky. In his own words "It was the most anxious part of the flight, as I had no certainty that my direction was correct." And he did go adrift – a strong wind blew the little monoplane off course. But Blériot sighted the English coast in time to turn toward Dover, where he could see battleships in the harbor.

Flying closer, Blériot spotted his friend Monsieur Fontaine on top of the cliffs, waving a big French flag to show the best spot to land. Blériot circled twice to lose height and made a heavy landing but climbed out unhurt. The epic flight was over.

He was greeted by Fontaine and a Daily Mail reporter and later had an enthusiastic reception from excited crowds in London.

The saddest man of the day was Hubert Latham who tried the Channel crossing a week before. He was ready for another attempt only to be beaten at the start by Blériot.

▽ Unlike Latham, Blériot had no mechanical trouble on his flight. The following year, on June 2, 1910, Charles Rolls (of Rolls-Royce fame) flew the Channel twice on a nonstop return flight to Calais from Dover.

The first-ever air crossing of the Channel had been way back on January 7, 1785, when two balloonists, Jean-Pierre Blanchard and John Jefferies, made the trip in a hydrogen balloon. The flight took 2½ hours.

The first air show

In 1909, to celebrate the advance of aviation, France threw a week-long air show near Reims in the Champagne region of France.

The Wright brothers couldn't come to the show, but many other famous flyers were there including Henry Farman, who flew his own machine. In it, he won the Grand Prize by making the longest flight, more than 180 km (112 miles). Glenn Curtiss from the United States won two speed prizes in his *Golden Flier*. Louis Blériot won a speed prize in his Blériot XII, but later crashed in it.

Weather was poor during air show week and strong winds made flying difficult for many of the more delicate aircraft. But no one was seriously hurt and the show marked aviation as a serious industry.

Of the 38 aircraft which entered the show, only 23 actually made it into the air, but the idea of the event as a showcase for the young aviation industry was a real success. Air shows are now popular the world over, for selling aircraft and for entertainment.

▷ *The Golden Flier was flown by Glenn Curtiss. Its wheeled undercarriage had a tricycle layout, an arrangement that has since become almost universal. Curtiss later designed many successful aircraft, including seaplanes. His flying boats were used in 1919 by the US Navy in the first air crossing of the Atlantic Ocean.*

Though the Wrights were not at Reims, several of their machines were at the meeting. On the far right here is a Wright A, flown by Eugène Lefebvre.

△ Hubert Latham had more luck at Reims than at Calais. He flew this Antoinette to a prize-winning height of 155 m (508 ft).

△ The Blériot XII was less elegant than the plane he used to cross the English Channel.

▷ The Henry Farman III in which he won the distance prize. It had large ailerons for good roll control.

Across the Mediterranean Sea

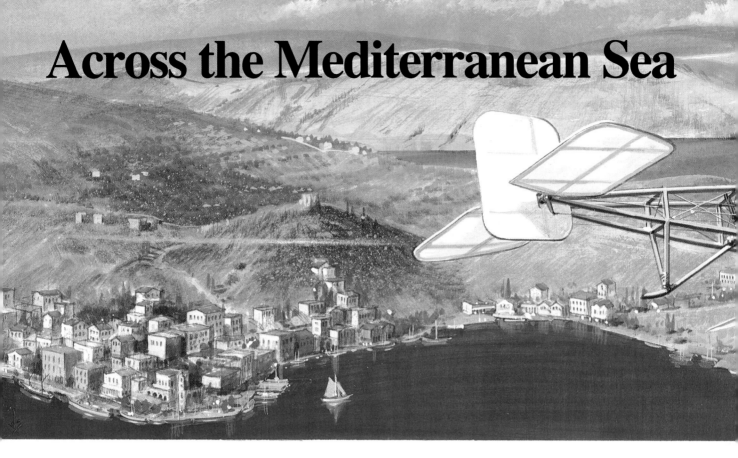

R oland Garros was born on the island of Réunion in the Indian Ocean. In 1908, when he was 20 years old, he arrived in Paris for classical piano studies. But Garros saw Santos-Dumont giving a flying display, fell in love with aviation and spent the piano tuition money learning to fly.

Garros soon flew as well as he played the piano, and in 1910 he competed with a French team in the Statue of Liberty air races in New York, finishing in third place. His ambition was to fly from France, across the Mediterranean Sea, to North Africa. The distance was nearly 800 km (500 miles) which would be a great test of aircraft reliability.

At 5.45 am on September 23, 1913, Garros took off from Fréjus aerodrome in the south of France. Heading out across the sea, he first aimed for the island of Sardinia, intending to land at the town of Cagliari to refuel. But as

△ *Weather on the flight was fine and clear. Here, Garros flies over the island of Sardinia, half way between France and the African coast.*

Garros soared high above the rugged hills of Sardinia, he decided that the Morane Saulnier monoplane was going so well that he wouldn't bother to land, calculating that there was just enough fuel to reach Africa non-stop.

French navy motor torpedo boats were on patrol in case he came down in the water, but they weren't needed. Eight hours after takeoff Garros made a safe landing at Bizerta in Tunisia. The little plane had averaged a speed of 92 km/h (57.5 mph), an excellent performance over the 738-km (458-mile) flight. Garros had certainly worked out his fuel reserves with precision – there were just five liters (1.3 US gallons) of fuel left in the tank when he switched off the motor.

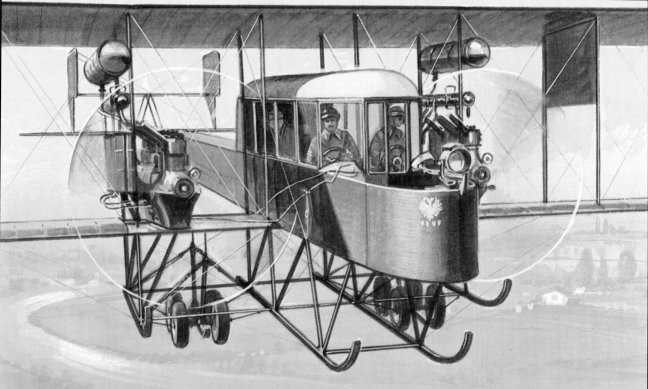

The Russian designer Igor Sikorsky, later to become famous for his helicopters, had an obsession with size. Unlike most other designers, Sikorsky thought BIG. His giant Russkiy Vitiaz had four engines mounted behind each other in pairs. It was the first successful big aircraft, and flew in May 1913. A year later, after the outbreak of World War I, Sikorsky bombers became stars of the fledgling Russian air force.

The dream come true

World War I started less than a year after the Mediterranean flight of Roland Garros. During this war, aircraft were developed into tough and deadly weapons. But despite technical developments, the dream of spreading your wings and flying like a bird was as far away as ever. It wasn't until the 1970s that man-powered flight became possible.

The design of a successful man-powered aircraft (MPA) was spurred on by prizes offered by Henry Kremer, a rich industrialist. In 1977, the *Gossamer Condor* was flown on a figure eight course to win a large sum for its designer, Dr Paul MacCready. Then MacCready and his team decided to build another MPA to try a Channel flight 70 years after Blériot's first triumphant crossing.

The design of the Channel flyer, named *Gossamer Albatross*, made use of the latest lightweight plastic and carbon fiber materials. In all, the MPA weighed in at just 39 kg (86 lb), despite having a wingspan as big as a medium sized airliner! The pilot sat on a bicycle seat and pedaled along. The pedals turned a 4.1 m (13 ft 6 in) propeller which gave the plane a speed of about 19 km/h (12 mph). In some ways, the design of *Gossamer Albatross* echoed that of the Wright *Flyer*: it had a pusher propeller, front-mounted elevator and used wing-warping for roll control.

At 5.51 am on June 12, 1979, Bryan Allen, a professional cyclist, pedaled the *Albatross* off a hardboard and concrete launch pad set under the cliffs of Dover. His target was the beach at Wissant in France. The sea was smooth and calm as Allen piloted the plane 4.6 m (15 ft) above the surface. For an hour he made good time, then headwinds reduced his progress to a slow and exhausting pace. The crew of one of the accompanying speedboats prepared to tow the plane by extending

a rod and line, but then Allen felt a change in the wind and shouted "Don't hook up yet!" He had to shout as his radio had failed 20 minutes after takeoff. Then a huge supertanker came up dead ahead, but just in time, Dover coastguards sent a radio message and ordered the ship to change course.

By 7.50 am the batteries that powered the altimeter and airspeed indicator were starting to fade and Allen was tiring as well. He could see no sign of the French coast – in fact seeing anything outside was difficult as

the clear plastic skin of the plane was covered in moisture. Then Allen saw a lighthouse looming out of the sea mist and despite cramps in both legs, he kept pedaling, knowing the beach couldn't be far away. But it wasn't until 8.40 am that Allen finally pedaled the *Albatross* over the rocks and surf to the sandy beach at Wissant.

▽ Bryan Allen sat below the wing on a tube framework like that of a bicycle. He sat inside a clear plastic housing which doubled as a fin to help stability.

A chain drive from the pedals turned the propeller. For the flight MacCready's team took a Kremer prize of £100,000 British pounds.

Aircraft data

Here are the main types of aircraft described in this book, drawn to the same scale. There are no accurate records of the earliest types so the pictures of these are based on expert estimates. These early aircraft were made of fairly similar materials. The structure was of wood or light metal tubing, covered with thin fabric. This was doped to stretch it tight and make it resist fuel spills and water vapor.

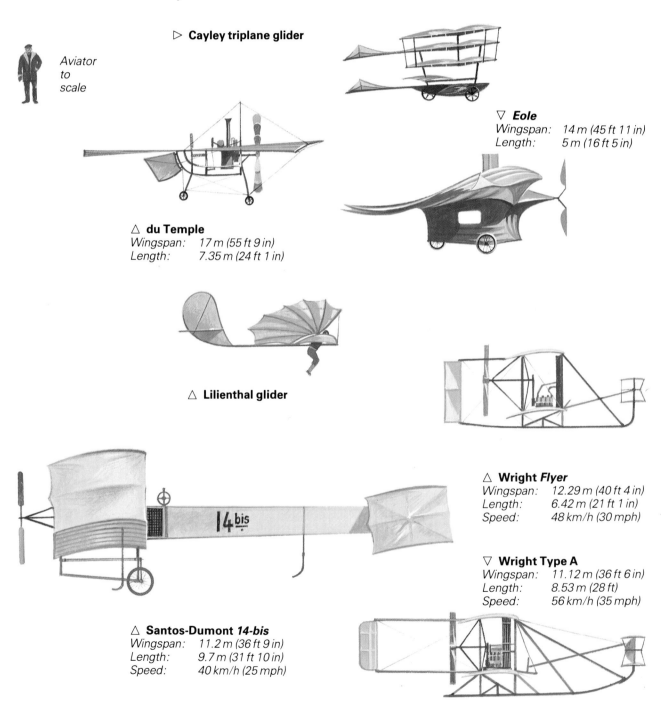

Aviator
to
scale

▷ **Cayley triplane glider**

▽ *Eole*
Wingspan: 14 m (45 ft 11 in)
Length: 5 m (16 ft 5 in)

△ **du Temple**
Wingspan: 17 m (55 ft 9 in)
Length: 7.35 m (24 ft 1 in)

△ **Lilienthal glider**

△ **Wright *Flyer***
Wingspan: 12.29 m (40 ft 4 in)
Length: 6.42 m (21 ft 1 in)
Speed: 48 km/h (30 mph)

▽ **Wright Type A**
Wingspan: 11.12 m (36 ft 6 in)
Length: 8.53 m (28 ft)
Speed: 56 km/h (35 mph)

△ **Santos-Dumont *14-bis***
Wingspan: 11.2 m (36 ft 9 in)
Length: 9.7 m (31 ft 10 in)
Speed: 40 km/h (25 mph)

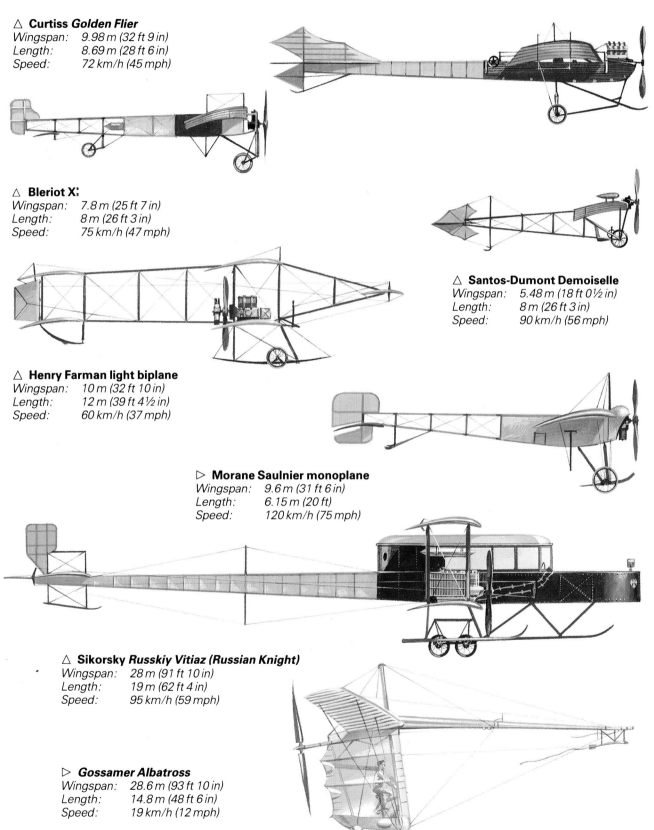

▽ **Levasseur Antoinette**
Wingspan: 12.8 m (42 ft)
Length: 11.5 m (37 ft 9 in)
Speed: 70 km/h (43.5 mph)

△ **Curtiss** *Golden Flier*
Wingspan: 9.98 m (32 ft 9 in)
Length: 8.69 m (28 ft 6 in)
Speed: 72 km/h (45 mph)

△ **Bleriot XI**
Wingspan: 7.8 m (25 ft 7 in)
Length: 8 m (26 ft 3 in)
Speed: 75 km/h (47 mph)

△ **Santos-Dumont Demoiselle**
Wingspan: 5.48 m (18 ft 0½ in)
Length: 8 m (26 ft 3 in)
Speed: 90 km/h (56 mph)

△ **Henry Farman light biplane**
Wingspan: 10 m (32 ft 10 in)
Length: 12 m (39 ft 4½ in)
Speed: 60 km/h (37 mph)

▷ **Morane Saulnier monoplane**
Wingspan: 9.6 m (31 ft 6 in)
Length: 6.15 m (20 ft)
Speed: 120 km/h (75 mph)

△ **Sikorsky** *Russkiy Vitiaz (Russian Knight)*
Wingspan: 28 m (91 ft 10 in)
Length: 19 m (62 ft 4 in)
Speed: 95 km/h (59 mph)

▷ *Gossamer Albatross*
Wingspan: 28.6 m (93 ft 10 in)
Length: 14.8 m (48 ft 6 in)
Speed: 19 km/h (12 mph)

Principles of flight

Four forces act on an aircraft in flight. Thrust from its propellers (or jets in a modern aircraft) makes it move forward. Air flowing over the wings generates lift to keep the plane aloft. Against these two forces are weight, which gravity pulls downward and drag, which slows the aircraft. When the engines no longer provide thrust, drag slows the plane down and the force of gravity brings it back to earth again.

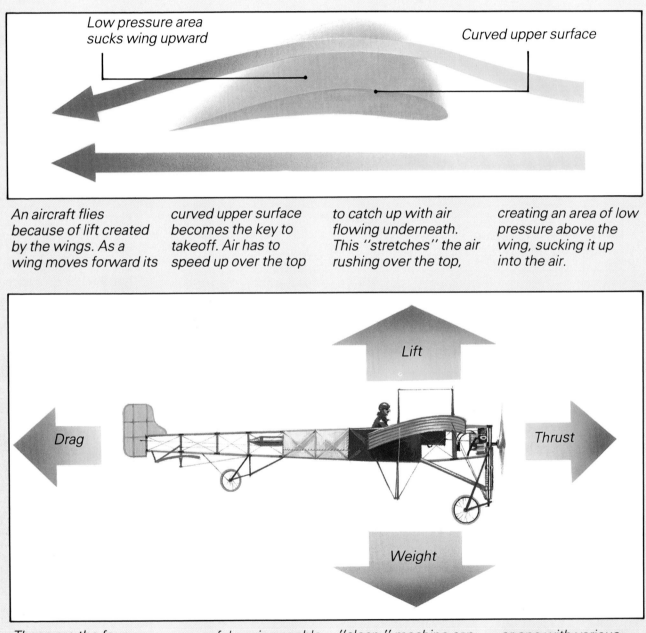

Low pressure area sucks wing upward

Curved upper surface

An aircraft flies because of lift created by the wings. As a wing moves forward its curved upper surface becomes the key to takeoff. Air has to speed up over the top to catch up with air flowing underneath. This "stretches" the air rushing over the top, creating an area of low pressure above the wing, sucking it up into the air.

Lift

Drag

Thrust

Weight

These are the four forces which act on an aircraft in the air. Lightness and a powerful engine enable an aircraft to take off in a short distance. A smoothly designed, "clean," machine can slip through the air more easily than one with a boxy shape or one with various pieces of equipment sticking out into the airflow.

Glossary

Airship
Cigar-shaped gas balloon fitted with motor and propeller. The earliest types used steam engines, but other engines can be used. The first airship was flown by Henry Giffard in 1852, but it was not powerful enough to fly into a strong head wind.

Airspeed indicator
Instrument that measures an aircraft's speed through the air.

Altimeter
Instrument that measures an aircraft's altitude.

Biplane
An aircraft with two sets of wings, one above the other. A monoplane has one set of wings, while a triplane has a deck of three.

Carbon fiber
Modern material that combines light weight with great strength.

Control surface
Any of several parts of an aircraft that stick out into the airflow to make the plane roll (bank), climb, dive or turn. Ailerons control bank. Elevators make the nose rise or fall (pitch) and a rudder controls the side to side angle (yaw).

Roll

Pitch

Yaw

Fuselage
The main body of an aircraft. The ''tail-plane'' includes the fin and rudder.

Heavier-than-air machine
An aircraft which does not make use of lifting gases.

Hot air balloon
A balloon that is filled with hot air, heated by a flame of some kind. The Montgolfier brothers used an open fire. Hot air rises as it is less dense than cooler air, so the balloon goes up. A gas balloon is filled with a gas such as hydrogen or helium.

Internal combustion engine
Engine similar to that used in, for example, a modern automobile. A gasoline and air mixture is ignited in a cylinder to make a piston move up and down at high speed. The piston is connected to a rotating rod, to which can be added wheels or propellers.

Takeoff track
The Wright brothers used a wooden rail track for the Flyer and the Type A. This was so the skid under-carriage would not dig into the ground when gaining speed.

Trailing edge
Rear edge of a wing. The front is called the leading edge.

Undercarriage
The wheels, skids or skis which a plane uses while on the ground.

Wind tunnel
Device used to test aircraft. Can be small for model testing or large enough for full-sized aircraft. All wind tunnels work in the same way. A powerful fan sends a stream of air along the tunnel and the effects of the airflow can be measured without having to make test flights first.

Index

PRINTED IN BELGIUM BY
proost
INTERNATIONAL BOOK PRODUCTION